philosophy

inspirational quotations and thoughts

Suzanne Maher

Illustrations by Cate Edwards

words to live by

First published August 2005
Second Edition February 2006
Copyright © Affirmations Australia Pty Ltd 2005

Published by
Affirmations Australia Pty Ltd
34 Hyde Street, Bellingen NSW 2454 Australia
Tel: (61 2) 6655 2350
Email: philosophy@affirmations.com.au
Web: www.affirmations.com.au

Designed by Suzanne Maher
Illustrations © Cate Edwards 2005, Bellingen, Australia
Edited by Barbara Maher

ISBN 0-9757703-0-6
Printed on recycled paper using vegetable based inks.
Printed in China

The chance discovery of nine journals, covered in dust
on a bookshelf in a tiny Australian country town,
led to the collaboration of drawings and enlightened messages in this book.

Hidden inside these journals were pages
of delightful illustrations, a soul's intimate journey through the
trials, hopes and revelations of life, waiting to be released into the world.

what we are about to undertake is an expedition together

a journey of discovery
into the most secret recesses of our consciousness

and for such an adventure we must travel light
we cannot burden ourselves with opinions
prejudices
conclusions
that is
with all the baggage that we have collected
over the past two thousand years or more

forget everything you know about yourself

forget everything that you have thought about yourself

we are going to set off
as if we know nothing

krishnamurti

life
is a
journey
and
love
is
what
makes
the
journey
worthwhile

you
will find
as you look
back upon your life
that the moments
when you have truly lived
are the moments
when you have done things
in the spirit of love

henry drummond

you do not need to leave your room

remain sitting at your table and listen
do not even listen
simply wait
do not even wait
be quite still and solitary
the world will freely offer itself to you
to be unmasked
it has no choice

it will roll in ecstasy at your feet

franz kafka

to lose
your way
is one way
of finding it

your daily life is your temple
and your religion
whenever you enter into it
take with it your all

k a h l i l   g i b r a n

leave
a
good
name
behind
you

attitude

catch the good that is within your reach
william james

happiness
sneaks in through a door
you didn't know
you had left open

john barrymore

if you learn
to laugh
at yourself
you will never
run out of material

helen keller

you are searching
the world
for treasure
but the real treasure
is yourself

nature is painting
for us day after day
pictures of infinite beauty
if only we had
eyes to see them

john ruskin

after

all

is

said

and

done

more

is

said

than

done

each individual
who takes responsibility
helps to make the world
a better place

open the window to your heart

simplicity
is
the
ultimate
sophistication

leonardo da vinci

teachers open the door

but you must enter by yourself

chinese proverb

believe

believe nothing
no matter where you read it
or who said it
not even if i said it
unless it agrees with
your own reason and
your own common sense

buddha

and
in
the dew
of little things
the heart
finds its morning
and is refreshed

kahlil gibran

the heart i

occasionally
what you
have to do
is go back
to the beginning
and see everything
in a new way

peter straub

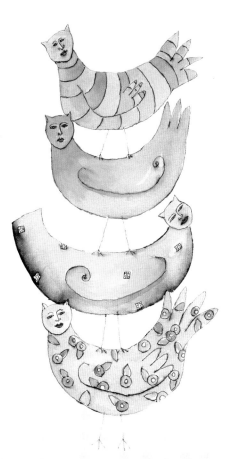

a mast

the art
of achievement
is the art
of making
your life
a masterpiece

erpiece

each
moment
of
your
life
is
a
brush
stroke
in
the
painting
of
your
growing
career

of all the people you will know in a lifetime
you are the only one you will never leave nor lose
to the question of your life you are the only answer
to the problems in your life you are the only solution

your mind is your garden
your thoughts are your seeds
you can grow flowers
or you can grow weeds

minds are like parachutes
they only function when open

thomas dewar

life is a

it is when you give
of yourself
that you truly give

kahlil gibran

life is a journey

we are all passengers
on a boat called life
and we are all alive
in the moment
called now

the journey of life
is so beautiful
that it needs
no destination

one

has

to

be

oneself

think deeply
speak gently
love much
laugh often
work hard
give freely
pay promptly
be kind

dismiss whatever insults your soul

let
life
flow
through
you

this
is
what
you
shall
do

everything is painted
with the brush
of the invisible One

let us follow
the hidden signs
and
find the Painter

r u m i

remember always
that you have
not only the right
to be an individual
you have an obligation to be one

you cannot make
any useful contribution
in life unless you do this

eleanor roosevelt

if you want peace
don't harbour bad thoughts
do not gossip
and
don't teach
what you do not know

r u m i

do not look back

no one knows how the world ever began

do not fear the future

nothing lasts forever

if you dwell on the past

or the future

you will miss

the moment

rumi

to find a pearl
dive deep
into the ocean
don't look in fountains

to find a pearl
you must
emerge from the water of life
always thirsty

i am forever unwrapping the eternal present

let
your
life
lightly
dance
on
the
edges
of
time
like dew on the tip of a leaf

rabindranath tagore

take only memories...

the longest journey
you will make
in your life
is from
your head
to your heart

sioux saying

your pain is the breaking
of the shell that encloses
your understanding

kahlil gibran

we

need

never

be

afraid

of

our

tears

charles dickens

the purpose of life
is to be useful
to be responsible
to be honourable
to be compassionate
it is after all
to matter
to count
to stand for something
to have made some difference
that you lived at all

leo roston

when you can do the common things in life
in an uncommon way
you command
the attention
of the
world

only
those
who
risk
going
too
far
can
possibly
find
out
how
far
one
can
go

t s eliot

i am only one

but i am still one
i cannot do everything
but still
i can do something

i will not refuse to do the something
i can do

helen keller

there are moments when we touch one another

everything

they are the moments

joy

is not in things
it is in us

richard wagner

precisely the least

the softest

lightest

a lizards rustling

a breath

a breeze

a moments glance

it is little that makes the best happiness

seek the wisdom
that will untie
your knot

seek the path
that demands
your whole being

rumi

dream lofty dreams
and as you dream
so shall you become

john ruskin

if we go down deep
into ourselves
we find that
we possess
exactly
what we desire

simone weil

when you get into a tight place
and everything goes against you
till it seems as though you could not
hang on a minute longer
never give up

for that is just the place
and time
that the tide will turn

harriet beecher stowe

the bird of vision
is flying towards you
with the wings of desire

rumi

throw
your
heart
out
in
front
of
you
and
run
ahead
to
catch
it

arab proverb

the moment you have in your heart
this extraordinary thing called love
and feel the depth
the delight
the ecstasy of it
you will discover
that for you
the world is
transformed

krishnamurti

all that we are

is

a

result

of

what

we

have

thought

buddha

every object
every being
is a jar
full
of
delight

rumi

beauty
is not
in the face

it is
a light
in the heart

kahlil gibran

openness and honesty will bring us
the love we deserve

once you make a decision
the universe conspires
to make it happen

ralph waldo emerson

when patterns are broken
new
worlds
emerge

tuli kupferberg

look famous be legendary appear complex act eas

diate presence   travel light   seem a dream   prove real

let us enjoy
this fleeting moment

omar khayyam

simplify

stop bothering
with non-essentials

it is time now
for trees
and grass
and growing things

we find in life exactly what we put into it

ralph waldo emerson

if you
can
dream it
you
can
make
it so

thoreau

your heart can guide you home

rumi

life
can
only
be
understood
backwards
but
must
be
lived
forwards

soren kierkegaard

one
word
frees
us

and that word is love

sophocles

tell me who admires and loves you
and i will tell you who you are

charles augustin sainte-beuve

joy is a net of love that catches souls

mother teresa

it is not only necessary
to love
it is also necessary
to say so

french proverb

love truth
and
pardon error

voltaire

the best portion
of a good life
is the little nameless
unremembered acts of kindness
and
of love

william wordsworth

tomorrow is a new day

begin it well
and serenely
and with spirit

ralph waldo emerson

write it on your heart
that every day
is the best day
of the year

ralph waldo emerson

if you want to be happy

be

leo tolstoy

make your mental garden beautiful

we should learn
to live simply
and by
one common principle

looking out
for one another

it makes
absolutely
no
difference
whatsoever
what
people
think
of
you

r u m i

do what you do

best

in order to be irreplaceable
one must always
be different

coco chanel

it's not what you look at
that matters
it's what you see

thoreau

there
is
only
one
moment
in
time
when
it
is
essential
to awaken

that moment is now

buddha

life
is an experiment

the journey
is
the
reward

let yourself
be silently drawn
by the strange
pull
of what
you really love

it will not
lead you astray

rumi

the
quieter
you
become
the
more
you
can
hear

baba ram das

hear blessings
dropping their blossoms
around you

rumi

i saw an angel in the marble and carved until i set her free

michaelangelo

the truth

you are
the truth
from foot to brow

now what else
would you like to know?

rumi

if you want to be someone   be yourself

keep yourself
clean and bright
you are the window
through which
you must see the world

george bernard shaw

it is not important what you believe
only
that you believe

the whole world is pulsing
with the power of the infinite
wave after wave of bliss
your heart is like the shore
and the ocean of infinite love
is breaking on the shores
of your heart

paramahansa yogananda

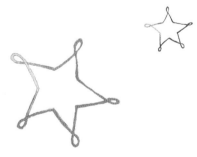

learn to be calm
and you will always
be happy

paramahansa yogananda

shakespeare

the biggest room
in the world
is the room for
improvement

find a seed
at the bottom of your heart
and bring forth
a flower

shigenori kameoka

a single moment of understanding can flood a whole life with meaning

humility

i
am
still
learning

michaelangelo

if you do not change direction
you will end up where you are going

lao tzu

life is not measured by the number of breaths we take

but by the number of moments that take our breath away

and forget not that the earth
delights to feel your bare feet
and the winds long
to play with your hair

kahlil gibran

look up and not down
look out and not in
look forward and not back
and lend a hand

edward everett hale

when you have
come to the end
of all the light you have
and you must step
into the darkness

be sure
of one of two things

either you will find
something firm to stand on
or
you will be taught
to fly

let your enthusiasm radiate
in your voice
your actions
your facial expressions
your personality
the words you use
and the thoughts you think

nothing great was ever achieved
without enthusiasm

ralph waldo emerson

be
the change
you want
to see
in
the
world

g a n d h i

a dream is a wish your heart makes

today a bird showed me the way

led me to the shore
of the ocean of joy

suddenly
i saw the sun

suddenly
my soul opened

rabindranath tagore

With special thanks to Barbara Maher.

While every effort has been made to acknowledge the author of the quotations used, please notify the publisher if this has not occurred.